CONNECT BIBLE STUDIES

Harry Potter and the Goblet of Fire

By J K Rowling (Bloomsbury, 2000)

Magic
Adolescence
Ambition
Good and Evil

www.connectbiblestudies.com

connect

linking the Word to the world

CONNECT BIBLE STUDIES: Harry Potter and the Goblet of Fire

Published in this format by Scripture Union, 207-209 Queensway, Bletchley, MK2 2EB, England.

Scripture Union is a charitable organisation working around the world with the goal of making God's good news known to people of all ages and encouraging them to meet God regularly through the Bible and prayer. As well as publishing books, Bible reading notes, and a range of church resources, SU produces videos and audio cassettes, works in schools, and runs holidays, clubs and missions for children and young people.

Email: info@scriptureunion.org.uk
Internet: www.scriptureunion.org.uk

© Damaris Trust, PO Box 200, Southampton, SO17 2DL.

Damaris Trust enables people to relate Christian faith and contemporary culture. It helps them to think about the issues within society from a Christian perspective and to explore God's truth as it is revealed in the Bible. Damaris provides resources via the Internet, workshops, publications and products.

Email: office@damaris.org
Internet: www.damaris.org

ALSO AVAILABLE AS AN ELECTRONIC DOWNLOAD: www.connectbiblestudies.com

Chief editor: Nick Pollard
Consultant Editor: Andrew Clark
Managing Editor: Di Archer
Written by Di Archer, Caroline Puntis, Tony Watkins

First published 2001
ISBN 1 85999 578 0

British Library Cataloguing-in-Publication Data: a catalogue record for this book is available from the British Library.

Cover design and print production by:
CPO, Garcia Estate, Canterbury Road, Worthing, West Sussex BN13 1BW.

Other titles in this series:

And more titles following — check www.connectbiblestudies.com for latest titles or ask at any good Christian bookshop.

linking the Word to the world

Using Connect Bible Studies

What Are These Studies?

These innovative home group Bible studies have two aims. Firstly, we design them to enable group members to dig into their Bibles and get to know them better. Secondly, we aim to help members to think through topical issues in a Biblical way. Hence the studies are based on a current popular book or film etc. The issues raised by these are the subjects for the Bible studies.

We do not envisage that all members will always be able to watch the films or read the books, or indeed that they will always want to. A summary is always provided. However, our vision is that knowing about these films and books empowers Christians to engage with friends and colleagues about them. Addressing issues from a Biblical perspective gives Christians confidence that they know what they think, and can bring a distinctive angle to bear in conversations.

The studies are produced in sets of four — i.e. four weeks' worth of group Bible Study material. These are available in print published by Scripture Union from your local Christian bookshop, or via the Internet at www.connectbiblestudies.com. Anyone can sign up for a free monthly email newsletter that announces the new studies and provides other information (sign up on the Connect Bible Studies website at www.connectbiblestudies.com/uk/register).

How Do I Use Them?

We design the studies to stimulate creative thought and discussion within a Biblical context. Each section therefore has a range of questions or options from which you as leader may choose in order to tailor the study to your group's needs and desires. Different approaches may appeal at different times, so the studies aim to supply lots of choice. Whilst adhering to the main aim of corporate Bible study, some types of questions may enable this for your group better than others — so take your pick.

Group members should be supplied with the appropriate sheet that they can fill in, each one also showing the relevant summary.

Leader's notes contain:

1.   Opening Questions

These help your group settle in to discussion, whilst introducing the topics. They may be straightforward, personal or creative, but are aiming to provoke a response.

2.   Summary

We suggest the summary of the book or film will follow now, read aloud if necessary. There may well be reactions that group members want to express even before getting on to the week's issue.

3.   Key Issue

Again, either read from the leader's notes, or summarised.

4.   Bible Study

Lots of choice here. Choose as appropriate to suit your group — get digging into the Bible. Background reading and texts for further help and study are suggested, but please use the material provided to inspire your group to explore their Bibles as much as possible. A concordance might be a handy standby for looking things up. A commentary could be useful too. The idea is to help people to engage with the truth of God's word, wrestling with it if necessary but making it their own.

Don't plan to work through every question here. Within each section the two questions explore roughly the same ground but from different angles or in different ways. Our advice is to take one question from each section. The questions are open-ended so each ought to yield good discussion — though of course any discussion in a Bible study may need prompting to go a little further.

5.   Implications

Here the aim is to tie together the perspectives gained through Bible study and the impact of the book or film. The implications may be personal, a change in worldview, or new ideas for relating to non-churchgoers. Choose questions that adapt to the flow of the discussion.

6.   Prayer

Leave time for it! We suggest a time of open prayer, or praying in pairs if the group would prefer. Encourage your members to focus on issues from your study that had a particular impact on them. Try different approaches to prayer — light a candle, say a prayer each, write prayers down, play quiet worship music — aim to facilitate everyone to relate to God.

7.   Background Reading

You will find links to some background reading on the Connect Bible Studies website: www.connectbiblestudies.com/

8.   Online Discussion

You can discuss the studies online with others on the Connect Bible Studies website at www.connectbiblestudies.com/discuss/

Scriptures referred to are taken from the Holy Bible, New International Version (NIV). Copyright (c) 1973, 1978, 1984 by International Bible Society. Other Bible translations can, of course, be used for the studies and having a range of translations in a group can be helpful and useful in discussion.

linking the Word to the world

Harry Potter and the Goblet of Fire

By J K Rowling (Bloomsbury, 2000)

Part One: Magic

'I don't believe in the kind of magic that appears in my books ...'
J K Rowling interviewed in USA Weekend Online, 14/11/99

Please read Using Connect Bible Studies *before leading a Bible study using this material.*

Opening Questions

Choose one of these questions.

What is your favourite children's story and why?	Mime your favourite children's story for the group to guess
Why are fantasy stories appealing?	Are fairy stories just for children? Why or why not?

Summary

Apart from being the son of a wizard and a witch, Harry Potter is no ordinary boy. As a baby, he had his first terrible encounter with the evil Lord Voldemort (also known as 'You-Know-Who' by those who fear even his name), who killed his father and then turned on Harry. His mother gave her life to save her son, imbuing Harry with a mysterious power through this act of love. The curse Voldemort subsequently hurled at Harry rebounded, robbing him of his own dark powers and leaving Harry with a scar on his forehead in the shape of a bolt of lightning. Voldemort was reduced to nothing and went into hiding for many years.

In this fourth book, Lord Voldemort makes an unwelcome return to power, stopping at nothing to regain his strength. He makes sure that Harry is one of the contenders in a tricky tournament that takes place at Harry's school, involving a series of difficult and sometimes life-threatening tasks. One of his followers is disguised as a teacher at Hogwarts to ensure that Harry will get his hands on the cup — a single touch will transport him to a graveyard where Voldemort is waiting to take his blood. 'B-blood of the enemy ... forcibly taken ... you will ... resurrect your foe,' goes the spell. To prove that he has returned to full strength, Voldemort announces that he will kill Harry Potter in a magical duel. It takes all of Harry's skill and determination to conquer him in a spectacular battle.

Key Issue: Magic

The success of the Harry Potter series is beyond question. All the books have sold tens of millions of copies worldwide. Adults and children alike have been snapping them up, enjoying the blend of humour, adventure and surprise.

Where Christians start debating is, of course, over the magic. At a fundamental level, the Harry Potter stories are powerful tales of the classic good versus evil battle, where the good very clearly wins. However, Harry the hero is a wizard and he is at Hogwarts to learn how to use magic for good. Hence he and his friends attend classes on spells, use cauldrons, collect weird ingredients and wear black cloaks as school uniform. The clashes between the goodies and the baddies are fought in the realms of magic, with spells and counterspells flashing from their wands.

Given the popularity of these books, how do we respond as Christians? Do we condemn them because of the magic? Or will we read them ourselves, and to our children? If we want to be relevant to our culture, we cannot just ignore them, when people we know will be reading them. Does the use of witchcraft negate the good/evil storyline? Is there a balanced Christian approach to the thorny subject of witchcraft in fantasyland?

Bible Study

Choose one question from each section.

1. What are people looking for in the occult?

'My dears, it is time for us to consider the stars … Human destiny may be deciphered by the planetary rays, which intermingle …' (p. 176)

Leaders: People are looking for some kind of control — they either want to know the future or they want to influence the present in some way. This may well be because of a basic need for security. In addition people are aware of a spiritual dimension to life and are looking for spiritual solutions that work.

♦ Read Isaiah 47:8–15. What are people looking for in magic, divination, and other occult practices?

   Leaders: see also 1 Samuel 28:3–20.

♦ Read Acts 13:6–12. Why does Paul react so strongly against Elymas?

   Imagine that you are Sergius Paulus. What are you looking for in life that makes you have Elymas on your staff and want to listen to the visitors to Paphos, Barnabas and Saul? How do you feel about Elymas's response to them and what happened to him as a result?

   Leaders: Note that the second part of this question invites people to imagine something of the background behind what Luke records for us in Acts 13. Putting yourself in the position of a character in the narrative can be a helpful way of thinking about what was happening in that character's life. Bear in mind, though, that this is pure speculation.

2. Why is God so opposed to the occult?

… he couldn't help thinking about what she had just said to him. 'I fear the thing you dread will indeed come to pass …' (p. 177)

Leaders: The fundamental problem with all magic, divination, etc. is that it looks to other spiritual forces for resources rather than to God. This is the root of all sin. In particular, it stops people listening to God (see Isaiah 8:19–20) and obeying him. It therefore threatens the distinctiveness, purity and security of God's people — and hence in the Old Testament (where the people of God are a nation) has the strictest penalties associated with it.

- Read Deuteronomy 18:9–16. Why does God find occult practices detestable (think about Israel's relationship with their neighbours and with the Lord)? What is the basic sin that is being committed? Try to find other Bible passages that address this fundamental sin.

  Leaders: see also Isaiah 8:19–9:1; Micah 5:10–15; Malachi 3:5; Galatians 5:19–21; Revelation 18:21–24; 21:8; 22:15.

- Read Leviticus 20:6. Why is the prostitution metaphor so appropriate? What should our relationship to God be like?

  Leaders: see also Nahum 3:1–4.

3. What's going on?

He had long since come to the conclusion that her brand of fortune-telling was really no more than lucky guesswork and a spooky manner. (p. 177)

Leaders: Both Old and New Testaments see occult practices as a mixture of trickery and real power drawn from demonic beings. The Bible is clear that ultimately they all fail. The second of the questions in this section explores this and broadens out to consider other things we do which parallel occult practices in that they rely on resources other than God.

- Compare Acts 8:9–13 with Acts 13:9–10. How does the Bible view the reality and power of occult practices? Contrast this with the power of the Holy Spirit in both passages.

  Leaders: see also Jeremiah 27:8–10; Ezekiel 13:17–23.

- List some of the ways in which magic fails in Isaiah 47:8–15. Try to summarise this passage in your own words. Are there ways in which our actions and attitudes parallel those described here even if we don't actually engage in magic or sorcery?

4. But what about ...?

Except, of course, for that time at the end of last term, when she had made the prediction about Voldemort rising again ... and Dumbledore himself had said that he thought that trance had been genuine, when Harry had described it to him ... (p. 177)

Leaders: In the context of the Bible's condemnation of occult practices, there are a couple of surprises. First, Daniel ends up in an extraordinary position as 'chief of the magicians, enchanters, astrologers and diviners' (see Daniel 1:8, 17–20; 2:27; 4:4–9; 5:10–12). Second, God brings the Magi to worship the newborn Christ through their astrology. The Magi were the priestly caste of the Persian Empire and may have been the successors of those Daniel worked with — at least after the fall of Babylon to Persia. The Bible doesn't give us any explanation for these surprises. Therefore the following questions are largely speculative but it is, however, worth giving a little thought to why this might be so.

- Read Matthew 2:1. Discuss what reasons God *might* have had for choosing some Magi to come and worship the young Jesus.

- Read Daniel 1:1–7. Put yourself in Daniel's position in the first few days of his exile:
  - carried far away from home at a young age (maybe even as young as 13)
  - thrust into a vast, sophisticated, prosperous and very diverse city — Babylon
  - stripped of his cultural identity — e.g. given a new Babylonian name
  - forced to learn about Babylonian culture — full of idolatry and occult practices

  Read verses 8–21. How does Daniel respond? How do you think you would have responded?

  Daniel eventually became 'chief of the magicians, enchanters, astrologers and diviners' (Daniel 5:11). How do you think he was able to handle being a believer in God in such a position for all those years?

Implications

That feeling of looking forward to lunchtimes, so I could read Harry's world of magic, is great, so I'd like to thank you for adding that touch of excitement to my day. (12 year-old fan, inside cover)

Choose one or more of the following questions.

Leaders: Some of these implication questions arise directly from the Bible study. Others are more immediately connected with Harry Potter but should still be informed by what you have discussed from Scripture. Don't discuss all of them! Encourage your group to discuss these issues at a practical level, not just in an abstract, intellectual way. You may also like to suggest that the members of your group talk to a child about Harry Potter books during the coming week.

- In what ways have we tried to take control of our own lives rather than trusting God (whether occult dabblings or otherwise)?

- What would you say to someone who wants to go to or has been to see a medium, clairvoyant, tarot card reader or similar?

- In an interview with *USA Weekend Online* (14 November 1999), J K Rowling said, 'I don't believe in the kind of magic that appears in my books but I do believe something very magical can happen when you read a good book.' How would you talk to a child about the Harry Potter books?

- How well do you think children are able to discern the difference between fantasy and reality? Should we be worried about children reading the Harry Potter books or are we simply projecting our own fears onto children?

- How would you explain the extraordinary fascination with Harry Potter? What are the implications of this for our evangelism?

Prayer

Spend some time praying through these issues.

Background Reading

You will find links to some background reading on the Connect Bible Studies website:
www.connectbiblestudies.com/uk/catalogue/0001/background.htm

Discuss

Discuss this study in the online discussion forums at www.connectbiblestudies.com/discuss

Members' sheet: Harry Potter & the Goblet of Fire — Part 1

Summary

Apart from being the son of a wizard and a witch, Harry Potter is no ordinary boy. As a baby, he had his first terrible encounter with the evil Lord Voldemort (also known as 'You-Know-Who' by those who fear even his name), who killed his father and then turned on Harry. His mother gave her life to save her son, imbuing Harry with a mysterious power through this act of love. The curse Voldemort subsequently hurled at Harry rebounded, robbing him of his own dark powers and leaving Harry with a scar on his forehead in the shape of a bolt of lightning. Voldemort was reduced to nothing and went into hiding for many years.

In this fourth book, Lord Voldemort makes an unwelcome return to power, stopping at nothing to regain his strength. He makes sure that Harry is one of the contenders in a tricky tournament that takes place at Harry's school, involving a series of difficult and sometimes life-threatening tasks. One of his followers is disguised as a teacher at Hogwarts to ensure that Harry will get his hands on the cup — a single touch will transport him to a graveyard where Voldemort is waiting to take his blood. 'B-blood of the enemy ... forcibly taken ... you will ... resurrect your foe,' goes the spell. To prove that he has returned to full strength, Voldemort announces that he will kill Harry Potter in a magical duel. It takes all of Harry's skill and determination to conquer him in a spectacular battle.

Key Issue

Bible Study notes

Implications

Prayer

www.connectbiblestudies.com

connect

linking the Word to the world

Harry Potter and the Goblet of Fire

By J K Rowling (Bloomsbury, 2000)

Part Two: Adolescence

'I will not be spoken to like that!' said Uncle Vernon, trembling with rage. (p. 35)

Please read Using Connect Bible Studies *before leading a Bible study using this material.*

Opening Questions

Choose one of these questions.

Do rules make you feel frustrated or safe?	When did you last break a rule? Why?
Are the Ten Commandments for everyone?	If you had to give one rule for the whole world, what would it be?

Summary

When Harry's scar hurts, it means that somewhere Lord Voldemort is active. In his dreams Voldemort's presence is almost real and Harry is soon convinced that he will suffer in Voldemort's planned return to power. Since his parents are dead, it is difficult for him to know whom to turn to for help. Harry has long since rejected the authority and 'stupid rules' of his guardians, the Dursleys, whose understanding of the world he lives in is minimal. 'What he really wanted (and it felt almost shameful to admit it to himself) was someone like — someone like a *parent:* an adult wizard whose advice he could ask without feeling stupid, someone who cared about him, who had had experience of Dark Magic ...' (p. 25).

He decides to get in touch with his dad's faithful friend, Sirius, who unfortunately has been wrongly accused of a crime and has had to go into hiding. To see him, Harry must break the school rules. He is unaware that the headmaster, Dumbledore, is also in contact with Sirius and knows about Harry's troubles. He tries to hide the truth from him, assuming that Dumbledore's age and authority would make him unable to understand what a teenager is going through.

As far as the pupils are concerned, their school appears to be run by the kind of rules that you would find in any boarding school. There are, of course, strict rules about the use of magic, particularly during the school holidays when the children are released back into the Muggle community armed with potentially dangerous knowledge. Dumbledore, however, is not afraid to bend the rules in favour of doing the right thing, and often gives Harry plenty of leeway.

Key Issue: Teenage Troubles

Many of the issues Harry faces are relevant to Western teenage culture. While not many may attend traditional boarding schools, magical or otherwise, they do have to relate to authority figures in teachers and parents. This is reportedly a vexing problem in some schools and homes, as the erstwhile 'children should be seen and not heard approach' bites the dust. What is the Biblical approach to human authority? Why should teens obey anyone? Is there an answer to the postmodern 'do as you like as long as it does not hurt anyone' tenet? Intergenerational issues are obviously important here, as is the powerful influence of a culture that minimises the inevitability of consequences. 'Because I say so' just does not seem to work anymore — why? What is the problem with obeying rules?

Bible Study

Leaders: Adolescence as a stage in life is not clear in the Bible. This is partly because people were generally married quite early. In Jesus' time, girls as young as twelve could be married. Boys came of age at thirteen and could take full responsibilities in the community. The rabbis seemed to think that the late teens was a good time for a young man to marry. In contemporary western societies adolescence is rather protracted due to earlier onset of puberty, marrying later in life and a longer time spent in education rather than working for a living.

Choose one question from each section.

1. Relationships across generations

Uncle Vernon closed the door sharply behind both of them. 'So,' he said, marching over to the fireplace and turning to face Harry as though he was about to pronounce him under arrest. 'So.' Harry would dearly loved to have said 'So what?', but he didn't feel that Uncle Vernon's temper should be tested this early in the morning ... (p. 31–32)

Leaders: The Bible puts a high priority on family relationships. The principle of honouring parents is still vitally important — but what does it look like in practice, especially when parents don't understand their children's world?

♦ Read Ephesians 5:21; 6:1–4. What do you think is the difference — if any — between 'obeying parents' and 'honouring them'? How might parents and others in authority over young people exasperate them?

   Leaders: see also Colossians 3:20–21.

♦ Read Ephesians 5:21; 6:1–4. Why do you think honouring parents is likely to lead to the blessings indicated here (and in Exodus 20:12)? What do you think it means to honour parents in today's culture — especially if a child is not living with both natural parents?

2. Obeying the rules

'I will not be spoken to like that!' said Uncle Vernon, trembling with rage. But Harry wasn't going to stand for this. Gone were the days when he had been forced to take every single one of the Dursleys' stupid rules. (p. 35)

Leaders: Adolescence is a time when young people push at the boundaries as they forge their own sense of identity. They are starting to think for themselves and are inclined to see rules as oppressive. How does God view rules? Are there bigger things at stake than sticking to human regulations? See 1 Corinthians 9:19–23 for Paul's perspective.

♦ Read Psalm 119:41–48, 97–104. What connection does the Psalmist see between freedom and God's law? How does his commitment to God's law affect his relationships with other people?

♦ Read John 5:1–23. Imagine that you had been brought up as a Pharisee with an incredibly strict set of rules about what was and wasn't permissible on the Sabbath. How do you think you would feel about Jesus healing someone and encouraging him to carry his mat on the Sabbath? What similar situations do we face in our churches today?

Leaders: Remember that in a Jewish culture (as in many non-Western cultures today), sons did what their fathers did. A baker's son becomes a baker; a carpenter's son becomes a carpenter. This is very important for understanding v. 17–18 and the rest of the passage.

3. Respecting authority

'Who's he, to lecture me about being out of bounds?' said Harry in mild indignation, as he folded up Sirius' letter and put it inside his robes. 'After all the stuff he did at school!' (p. 497)

Leaders: Respect for human authorities shows our respect for God's authority, since they are subject to God's authority themselves. The first human authority we have to contend with is that of our parents.

♦ Read Luke 2:41–52. What do we learn from this passage about how Jesus saw his relationship with his parents? How do you think Jesus' parents saw their relationship with him — both before and after they found him?

Leaders: see also Hebrews 5:8.

♦ Read Romans 13:1–7. How is our submission to God tied up with our submission to human authorities? What do you think this implies for the way we respond to authority that we don't like or agree with?

4. 'Spiritual adolescence'

'And then there was this big row,' Ginny said, 'because Mum wants them to go into the Ministry of Magic like Dad, and they told her all they want to do is open a joke-shop.' (p. 52)

Leaders: The Bible frequently uses physical development from birth to maturity as a metaphor for our spiritual development. Adolescents are immature but consider themselves to be mature, often have a weak sense of identity and are frequently rebellious. Perhaps there are some useful parallels between this stage of life and our spiritual immaturity.

♦ Read Hebrews 5:11–6:3. In what ways are we spiritually adolescent? What are some of the parallels between our spiritual immaturity and the immaturity of an adolescent young person? In what ways are they different?

♦ Read 1 Corinthians 13. In what ways is love the most important mark of real maturity in a believer? How does our spiritual immaturity show?

Leaders: Remember that the context of this passage is Paul rebuking the Corinthian church for its immaturity.

Implications

'That's not the point!' raged Mr Weasley. 'You wait until I tell your mother — ' (p. 51)

Choose one or more of the following questions.

♦ What steps do you need to take to improve your relationships with your parents or children (or with those who are either older or younger than yourselves)?

♦ How can you respond to those who say, 'I can do as I like as long as I don't hurt anyone'?

♦ What do you think about the portrayal of adolescence in the book? What more can your church do practically to help young people struggling with adolescence?

♦ What help do you need to be able to move beyond spiritual adolescence?

♦ Why do you struggle to obey certain rules? What are you going to do about it?

Prayer

Spend some time praying through these issues.

Background Reading

You will find links to some background reading on the Connect Bible Studies website:
www.connectbiblestudies.com/uk/catalogue/0001/background.htm

Discuss

Discuss this study in the online discussion forums at www.connectbiblestudies.com/discuss

Members' sheet: Harry Potter & the Goblet of Fire — Part 2

Summary

When Harry's scar hurts, it means that somewhere Lord Voldemort is active. In his dreams Voldemort's presence is almost real and Harry is soon convinced that he will suffer in Voldemort's planned return to power. Since his parents are dead, it is difficult for him to know whom to turn to for help. Harry has long since rejected the authority and 'stupid rules' of his guardians, the Dursleys, whose understanding of the world he lives in is minimal. 'What he really wanted (and it felt almost shameful to admit it to himself) was someone like — someone like a *parent*: an adult wizard whose advice he could ask without feeling stupid, someone who cared about him, who had had experience of Dark Magic ...' (p. 25).

He decides to get in touch with his dad's faithful friend, Sirius, who unfortunately has been wrongly accused of a crime and has had to go into hiding. To see him, Harry must break the school rules. He is unaware that the Headmaster, Dumbledore, is also in contact with Sirius and knows about Harry's troubles. He tries to hide the truth from him, assuming that Dumbledore's age and authority would make him unable to understand what a teenager is going through.

As far as the pupils are concerned, their school appears to be run by the kind of rules that you would find in any boarding school. There are of course strict rules about the use of magic, particularly during the school holidays when the children are released back into the Muggle community armed with potentially dangerous knowledge. Dumbledore, however, is not afraid to bend the rules in favour of doing the right thing, and often gives Harry plenty of leeway.

Key Issue

Bible Study notes

Implications

Prayer

Harry Potter and the Goblet of Fire

By J K Rowling (Bloomsbury, 2000)

Part Three: Ambition

'This whole Tournament's supposed to be about getting to know foreign wizards and making friends with them!' said Hermione shrilly. 'No it isn't!' shouted Ron. 'It's about winning!' (p. 368)

Please read Using Connect Bible Studies *before leading a Bible study using this material.*

Opening Questions

Choose one of these questions.

When did you last fulfil an ambition?	What is the difference between ambition and dreams?
Is letting go of an ambition giving up?	Do you like ambitious people?

Summary

'Harry rolled over in bed, a series of dazzling new pictures forming in his mind's eye ... he had hoodwinked the impartial judge into believing he was seventeen ... he had become Hogwarts champion ... he was standing in the grounds, his arms raised in triumph in front of the whole school, all of whom were applauding and screaming ... he had just won the Triwizard Tournament. Cho's face stood out particularly clearly in the blurred crowd, her face glowing with admiration ...' (p. 169–170). For Harry, the fourth year is all about recognition — both from his contemporaries and a pretty girl who also happens to be a great player in the magic world's favourite sport of Quidditch.

Hermione's greatest concern is still her schoolwork, although she develops a keen interest in the rights of Winky the house-elf and with great determination sets about winning justice for these underprivileged creatures.

Meanwhile, Harry's other best friend, Ron Weasley, is once again relegated to existing in Harry's shadow. The last in a long line of brothers, Ron would like to be seen as something more than just another Weasley boy. For both Harry and Ron, it's a case of wanting what the other has — Ron would like to have money and be a hero; Harry would give anything to have the love and support of a family like Ron's. The two friends fall out when Ron's jealousy finally gets the better of him.

Key Issue: Ambition

Ambition is a key theme in the book. Once Harry knows about the Triwizard Tournament he wants to compete and win. Similarly, the game of Quidditch fires his ambition for glory and success. Personal danger is forgotten in the quest for victory. Hence Harry's heroes are those who shine in his favourite sport, and he wants to earn his place among them. Linked with dreams of winning are fears of failure of course, and Harry is no exception. What does the Bible say about ambition? Is all ambition selfish and self-seeking? Should we shun success in the eyes of the world? Does going God's way mean that we abandon such dreams? Are there biblical heroes who can help? Is our identity simply in what we achieve? How do we handle failure and disappointment?

Bible Study

1. Selfish ambition

'They're not stopping me entering,' said Fred stubbornly, also scowling at the top table. 'The champions'll get to do all sorts of stuff you'd never be allowed to do normally. And a thousand galleons prize money!' 'Yeah,' said Ron, a faraway look on his face. 'Yeah, a thousand Galleons ...' (p. 167)

Leaders: Human ambition is generally characterised by competition, greed, self-centredness, and disregard for others. The Bible insists that Christians should be different — characterised instead by humility.

♦   Read Mark 10:35–44. Why do you think James and John thought that they deserved the honour they were requesting? How might we make the same mistakes as James and John with our ambitions?

   Leaders: see Mark 1:16–20; 3:13–19; 9:2–10.

♦   Read James 3:13–18. How have you seen the side-effects of ambition that James talks about in your own experience? What do you think James sees as appropriate ambition? How do you think the world would view James' perspective?

   Leaders: see also Habakkuk 2:4–20.

2. Ambitious Christians?

They shared a wish, a hope, a dream,
They hatched a daring plan
To educate young sorcerers
Thus Hogwarts School began.
Now each of these four founders
Formed their own house, for each
Did value different virtues
In the ones they had to teach.
By Gryffindor, the bravest were
Prized far beyond the rest;
For Ravenclaw, the cleverest
Would always be the best;
For Hufflepuff, hard workers were
Most worthy of admission;
And power-hungry Slytherin
Loved those of great ambition. (p. 157)

Leaders: Selfish ambition is not legitimate for Christians. However, there are legitimate ambitions, some of which Scripture insists on.

♦ Read Philippians 2:1–18; 3:12–14. What does Paul suggest are right ambitions for Christians? Does this rule out ambitions in our work or other parts of life?

♦ Read 2 Corinthians 5:11–21. How is our view of Christ, other people and ourselves different from that of a worldly point of view? How does that affect our ambitions and how we work towards them?

3. Failed ambitions

'Look,' said Hermione patiently, 'it's always you who gets all the attention, you know it is. I know it's not your fault,' she added quickly, seeing Harry open his mouth furiously, 'I know you don't ask for it ... but — well, you know, Ron's got all those brothers to compete against at home, and you're his best friend, and you're really famous — he's always shunted to one side whenever people see you, and he puts up with it, and he never mentions it, but I suppose this is just one time too many ...' (p. 254)

Leaders: Everyone has had the experience of frustration over ambitions that have not been reached, if not the disappointment of downright failure. How are we to handle this experience as Christians?

♦ Read 2 Corinthians 6:3–10. Do you think Paul experienced failure and disappointment when these things happened? How do you respond when your ambitions fail?

♦ Read Psalm 22:1–8. When life seems like it has fallen apart, what has happened to God's promises? How do we tell the difference between God's plans and ours?

4. How to achieve your ambitions

'I don't know what's going to happen to them, I really don't. No ambition, unless you count making as much trouble as they possibly can ...' (p. 55)

Leaders: The Bible is clear that it is God who enables us to achieve anything. Yet at the same time it expects us to work too and to be disciplined in striving after our ambitions.

♦ Read 2 Timothy 2:1–7. What's involved in the soldier, the athlete and the farmer attaining their ambitions? How do these apply to the Christian's life?

Leaders: When Paul writes about not getting 'involved in civilian affairs', he is not suggesting that we avoid people who aren't Christians — look at Paul's own ministry (Acts 17:16–34 for example) or Jesus' incarnation. Reaching the world is our mission.

♦ Read 2 Peter 1:3–8. How does this passage give us criteria against which to evaluate our ambitions and guidance for how to go about working towards them?

Implications

Normally, Uncle Vernon would have asked what car Mr Weasley drove; he tended to judge other men on how big and expensive their cars were. (p. 40)

Choose one or more of the following questions

♦ Is Harry Potter a good role model for children to learn about ambition?

♦ How honest have you been today about your ambitions? Are there some you need to let go of or to pursue?

♦ How would you try to help somebody who has been hit by disappointment — for example, a neighbour who has been passed over for promotion at work?

♦ What do you want to win at? How does the way you pursue this ambition need to change?

Prayer

Spend some time praying through these issues.

Background Reading

You will find links to some background reading on the Connect Bible Studies website: www.connectbiblestudies.com/uk/catalogue/0001/background.htm

Discuss

Discuss this study in the online discussion forums at www.connectbiblestudies.com/discuss

Members' sheet: Harry Potter & the Goblet of Fire — Part 3

Summary

'Harry rolled over in bed, a series of dazzling new pictures forming in his mind's eye ... he had hoodwinked the impartial judge into believing he was seventeen ... he had become Hogwarts champion ... he was standing in the grounds, his arms raised in triumph in front of the whole school, all of whom were applauding and screaming ... he had just won the Triwizard Tournament. Cho's face stood out particularly clearly in the blurred crowd, her face glowing with admiration ...' (p. 169–170). For Harry, the fourth year is all about recognition — both from his contemporaries and a pretty girl who also happens to be a great player in the magic world's favourite sport of Quidditch.

Hermione's greatest concern is still her schoolwork, although she develops a keen interest in the rights of Winky the house-elf and with great determination sets about winning justice for these underprivileged creatures.

Meanwhile, Harry's other best friend, Ron Weasley, is once again relegated to existing in Harry's shadow. The last in a long line of brothers, Ron would like to be seen as something more than just another Weasley boy. For both Harry and Ron, it's a case of wanting what the other has — Ron would like to have money and be a hero; Harry would give anything to have the love and support of a family like Ron's. The two friends fall out when Ron's jealousy finally gets the better of him.

Key Issue

Bible Study notes

Implications

Prayer

Discuss this with others on the Connect Bible Studies website: www.connectbiblestudies.com

Harry Potter and the Goblet of Fire

By J K Rowling (Bloomsbury, 2000)

Part Four: Good and Evil

'Remember, if the time should come when you have to make a choice between what is right, and what is easy, remember what happened to a boy who was good, and kind, and brave, because he strayed across the path of Lord Voldemort.' (p. 628)

Please read Using Connect Bible Studies *before leading a Bible study using this material.*

Opening Questions

Choose one of these questions.

Do you like happy endings? Why?	Do you see the glass half empty or half full?
Does every cloud have a silver lining?	Draw a picture of good versus evil

Summary

Mad-Eye Moody's Defence Against the Dark Arts class is designed to prepare the children for dealing with evil wizards who are likely to use magic immorally for their own selfish gain. The headmaster, Dumbledore, has given permission for the darkest curses of all to be demonstrated in class so that the pupils won't ever be taken by surprise. Moody is keen to ensure that Harry in particular is able to cope.

Harry has the chance to put his new skills to the test when once again he confronts Lord Voldemort. Voldemort's willingness to commit murder, starting with Harry's own parents when he was a baby, leaves the Dark Lord's evil nature in no doubt. His ravenous hunger for power knows no boundaries and he is unperturbed when he kills Harry's tournament rival, Cedric, whose presence threatens to scupper his plan.

Harry is invulnerable to Voldemort because of the love that Harry's mother demonstrated in dying to save her son, so Voldemort takes some of Harry's blood to give him protection too. In the final wand-to-wand battle, Voldemort is defeated by Harry, who is determined not to give up even though he thinks he might die. Harry escapes, mindful that a future encounter with Voldemort is inevitable.

Key Issue: Good versus evil

There is no doubt that good clearly defeats evil in the Harry Potter universe. However, the death of Cedric brings a sober note to this children's story. The victory was not without its cost. How far does this relate to the real world we live in? Do we see life in terms of a good/evil battle? What does it mean that Jesus has defeated the enemy? Do we have real casualties too? What does the Bible say about discernment over these issues? How do we know what is really going on?

Bible Study

1.   Knowing good and evil

'The only one against whom I intend to work,' said Dumbledore, 'is Lord Voldemort. If you are against him, then we remain, Cornelius, on the same side.' (p. 615)

Leaders: Throughout the Harry Potter books there is a clear distinction between good and evil. Although some characters who appear to be good turn out to be evil, they are not ultimately ambivalent. The Bible is similarly clear that the universe is moral with a real distinction between good and evil despite current claims that 'good' only has to be good for me.

♦   Read Genesis 3:1–13. How did Adam and Eve end up knowing good and evil in a way they didn't anticipate? How have we experienced a similar situation in our own lives?

♦   Read Ephesians 5:8–14. How can we discern good and evil? How might we work through the tension of having nothing to do with deeds of darkness but at the same time exposing them?

2.   Wisdom — living the good

'... Mr Potter was first to reach the hostages ... the delay in his return was due to his determination to return all hostages to safety, not merely his own ... Most of the judges ... feel that this shows moral fibre and merits full marks.' (p. 440)

Leaders: Wisdom in the Bible — especially in the Old Testament wisdom literature such as Proverbs — is not to do with intellectual knowledge but understanding how to live in the right way. In Proverbs wisdom is personified as a woman who invites people to learn from her. Folly, by contrast is living in rejection of wisdom and of God.

♦   Read Proverbs 9. How do the various images and metaphors in this passage work to illustrate and contrast wisdom and folly? What benefit or detriment comes through embracing wisdom or folly?

   Leaders: You may like members to share with the group times when they have experienced the gains or losses of embracing wisdom or folly in their own lives.

♦   Read Ephesians 5:1–21. Of all the instructions Paul gives us in the passage, which do you think is the most fundamental? Why? How should we respond to evil that we see in the world around us and in our own lives?

3. Saved through sacrifice

Voldemort said ... 'You all know that on the night I lost my powers and my body, I tried to kill him. His mother died in the attempt to save him ... His mother left upon him the traces of her sacrifice ... this is old magic, I should have remembered it.' (p. 566)

Leaders: When Harry Potter was a baby, Lord Voldemort tried to kill his family. However, Lord Voldemort's attempt to curse Harry rebounds onto him because Harry's mother had offered to die for him. Voldemort kills her anyway but her sacrifice protects Harry.

Both of the alternative questions here give group members an opportunity to reflect again on what Jesus' death achieved for us and to try to express this, since often Christians only have a hazy understanding of how his sacrifice accomplishes our salvation.

♦ Read Isaiah 53. Why did Jesus have to die? What does it mean to you?

   Leaders: see also Romans 5:6–8 and 1 Peter 3:18.

♦ Read 2 Corinthians 5:11–21. How does the 'great exchange' of verse 21 work? How should this affect the lives we live?

4. The final triumph of good

Voldemort and Wormtail had been talking about someone they had killed, though Harry could not remember the name ... and they had been plotting to kill someone else ... him ... (p. 21)

Leaders: Readers of the Harry Potter books hope that good will ultimately triumph but can have no reasonable certainty about this — apart from the realisation that this is children's fantasy literature. However, the Bible is clear that good has triumphed already in the cross, though the completion of the victory is still in the future.

♦ Read Psalm 73. Why is it important that we have the same perspective as the Psalmist about the certainty that God will deal with everything that is opposed to him? What do we need to be clear about in our minds in order to be able to have this perspective?

♦ Read Colossians 2:9–15. Paul says that the cross is Christ's ultimate victory over sin and satanic powers. From that point on Satan's downfall was inevitable yet until Christ returns to wind up history the 'powers and authorities' are still active in our world. How does the certainty of Christ's ultimate triumph affect our thinking and our day to day living?

   Leaders: A useful analogy for the current situation in which Christ has won the ultimate victory but all the consequences of that are still waiting to be worked out, is the D-Day invasion of 1944. Once the Allied forces held the Normandy beaches, Hitler's defeat was inevitable but there was still a long period of pressing on towards Berlin until the Victory was completed. (Remember, of course, that analogies are always imperfect and shouldn't be pushed too far!)

Implications

A wizard who's about to put an illegal curse on you isn't going to tell you what he's about to do. He's not going to do it nice and polite to your face. You need to be prepared. You need to be alert and watchful. (p. 187)

Choose one or more of the following questions

♦ If the battle has been won by Jesus, how does this affect your approach to conflict?

♦ 'There are two equal and opposite errors into which our race can fall about the devils. One is to disbelieve in their existence. The other is to believe, and to feel an excessive and unhealthy interest in them.' (C S Lewis, *The Screwtape Letters* [Fontana Books, 1971])
What is a balanced view of evil?

♦ How can the power of love be released in your life?

♦ Does the nature of the conflict between good and evil in the Harry Potter books outweigh the concerns about wizardry for you? How would you talk about this to a neighbour?

Prayer

Spend some time praying through these issues.

Background Reading

You will find links to some background reading on the Connect Bible Studies website:
www.connectbiblestudies.com/uk/catalogue/0001/background.htm

Discuss

Discuss this study in the online discussion forums at www.connectbiblestudies.com/discuss

Members' sheet: Harry Potter & the Goblet of Fire — Part 4

Summary

Mad-Eye Moody's Defence Against the Dark Arts class is designed to prepare the children for dealing with evil wizards who are likely to use magic immorally for their own selfish gain. The headmaster, Dumbledore, has given permission for the darkest curses of all to be demonstrated in class so that the pupils won't ever be taken by surprise. Moody is keen to ensure that Harry in particular is able to cope.

Harry has the chance to put his new skills to the test when once again he confronts Lord Voldemort. Voldemort's willingness to commit murder, starting with Harry's own parents when he was a baby, leaves the Dark Lord's evil nature in no doubt. His ravenous hunger for power knows no boundaries and he is unperturbed when he kills Harry's tournament rival, Cedric, whose presence threatens to scupper his plan.

Harry is invulnerable to Voldemort because of the love that Harry's mother demonstrated in dying to save her son, so Voldemort takes some of Harry's blood to give him protection too. In the final wand-to-wand battle, Voldemort is defeated by Harry, who is determined not to give up even though he thinks he might die. Harry escapes, mindful that a future encounter with Voldemort is inevitable.

Key Issue

Bible Study notes

Implications

Prayer

Discuss this with others on the Connect Bible Studies website: www.connectbiblestudies.com